Let's Be Indians

Let's Be Indians

by Peggy Parish

Drawings by Arnold Lobel

Harper & Row, Publishers

To
Mary
Fredda
and
Buddy
Parish

Contents

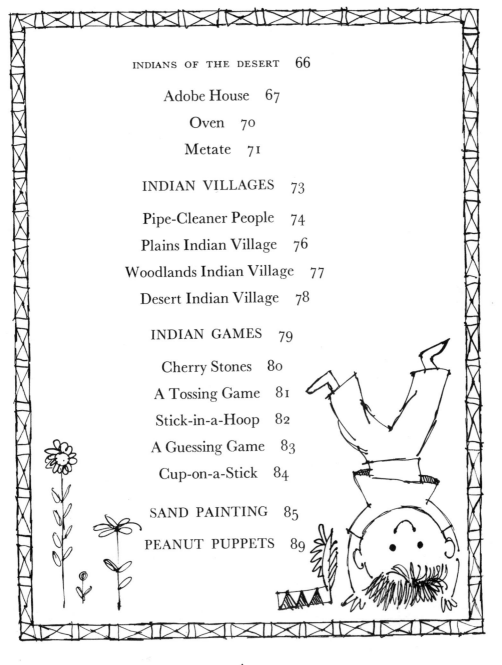

Introduction

Many years ago our country was quite different from the way it is today. There were no tall buildings, trains, cars, or planes. There were none of the man-made things which make up our life.

And there were not the many races of people we know. In this whole big country only one race of people lived—the Indians.

The Indians' way of life was completely different from ours, but they had the same needs that we have today. They needed food, clothing, a place to live, and ways to have fun. They had no stores from which to buy. They used just what they could find around them.

From this book you can learn a little about the way Indians in different parts of our country lived. You can learn how to make the kinds of things they used. Some of these things are large enough to use in playing your Indian games. Some are small models with which you can build Indian villages. Some are just for fun.

General Instructions

For the best results with these projects, you should:

1. Follow the instructions carefully.
2. Use a good all-purpose glue (Elmer's Glue-All, Sobo).
3. Use tempera paints. (These can be purchased at any stationery or dime store.)
4. Add a little liquid soap to the paint if you are going to paint a waxed or glossy surface.
5. Always wash your paintbrush well before you change to another color.

About Making Knots

For many of these projects rather large, tight knots are needed.

To make a knot:

1. Loop one end of the thread over, around, and under the thread.
2. Pull the ends of the thread to draw the loop into a knot.
3. Make another loop the same way.
4. Pull the second loop into a knot on top of the first.

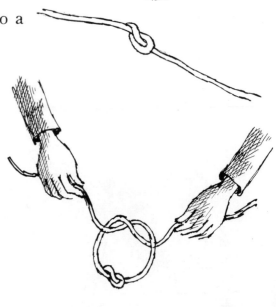

About Making Braids

Some of the projects call for braiding. The pictures will show you how to do this.

1. Divide the material into three parts as nearly equal as possible.

2. Bring an outside piece across the middle piece.

more

15

3. Bring the opposite outside piece across the middle piece.

4. Continue bringing outside pieces over the middle piece, working from first one side and then the other, until you have almost reached the end. Then tie the ends together with a small piece of yarn.

16

Recipe for Salt Clay

Salt clay is used for several projects. You can make some in advance and keep it stored in a plastic bag. Salt-clay objects will dry faster if placed near heat.

To make salt clay:

1. Mix one cup of flour with one cup of salt.

2. Add a little cool water and mix with your hands. If the mixture is too dry, add a little more water.

3. Mix until you have a ball of clay. This clay should be firm and not at all sticky. If it is sticky, add more flour.

Large Enough to Use

Headband

It is much more fun to pretend you are an Indian if you can dress like one and have the kinds of things Indians had to use. One of the first things you need to be an Indian is a headband.

1. Cut a strip of paper that is long enough to go around your head with two inches left over.

2. With crayons or paint put an Indian design around the headband.

3. Fit the band around your head, then staple or tape the ends in place.

4. Cut a piece shaped like a feather from colored paper. Cut out more feather-shaped pieces if you want more feathers in your head-band.

5. Cut short slits all around the piece of paper so it will look like a feather.

6. Staple or tape the paper feather in place.

Indian Costume

Most of the Indians' clothing was made from various kinds of animal skin. Deerskin made the nicest clothing. The women had no steel needles with which to sew. They punched holes with a sharp stone or bone. For thread they used animal tendons. Sewing was hard work. It took a long time to make a dress or shirt.

But you can make a fun Indian costume from an old sheet. Girls may use a loose-fitting bathrobe or nightgown for a pattern. Boys may use a loose-fitting pajama coat or a bathrobe and cut the costume a little shorter than the robe

1. Double the sheet and lay it flat. Lay the pattern (buttoned up) on the sheet so that the shoulder seams are on the fold and the sleeves are straight out. With a pencil mark where the hole for your head should be.

2. The sleeves of your pattern may not be exactly on the fold, but pretend they are and draw around the rest of

↿ *more* ⇁

the pattern. If you want shorter sleeves, mark them the length you think they should be.

3. Remove the pattern and cut along the lines. Be sure to cut through both layers of cloth.

4. Sew the bottoms of the sleeves and both sides of the costume.

5. Turn the costume so that the seams are on the inside.

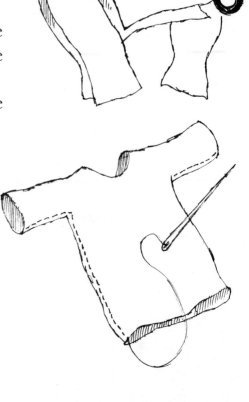

6. Cut slits around the ends of the sleeves and the bottom of the costume to make fringes. Crayon a bright Indian design on the costume.

7. If the hole for your head is not large enough, cut a slit in the middle of the back. This can be pinned when you wear the costume.

23

Moccasins

It was important that Indians walk quietly. If they were noisy while hunting, the animals would go away and the Indians would have no meat. As shoes, Indians wore soft moccasins made of animal skin. They often decorated the toes of the moccasins with porcupine quills or bright-colored beads. A good Indian wife kept several extra pairs of moccasins for each member of her family, as the moccasins wore out rather quickly.

You can make a pretend pair of moccasins from a pair of old socks.

1. Cut away the top part of the sock.

2. Fold a one-fourth-inch hem on the *outside* of the sock to make a casing for a draw-string.

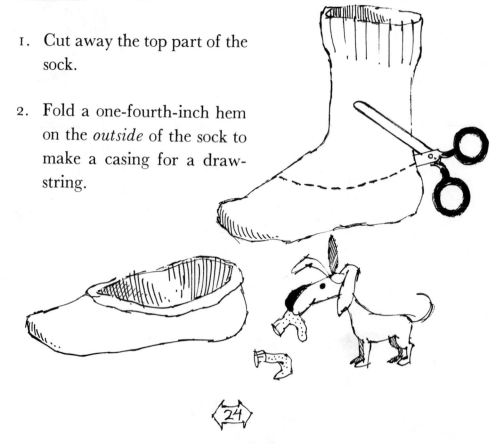

3. Starting almost at the center of the front, sew the hem down. Sew close to the bottom edge. Leave an opening in the center of the front large enough to insert a drawstring.

4. Cut a piece of colored yarn about twice as long as the moccasin to use as a drawstring. Starting at the center of the front, thread the drawstring through the casing. If you tie the string to a bobby pin or a safety pin, it will be easy to slip it around.

more

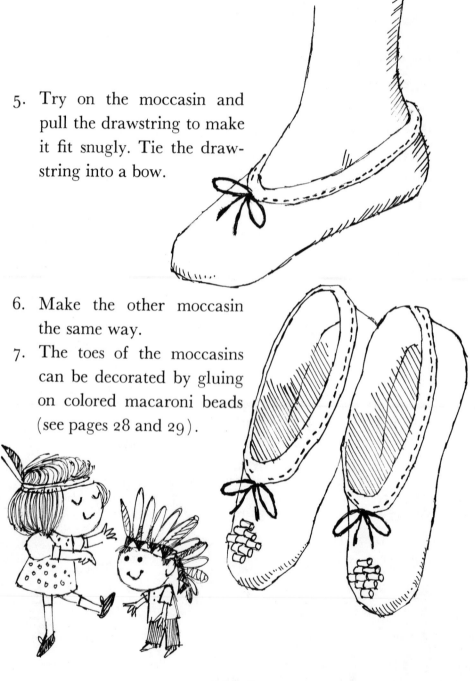

5. Try on the moccasin and pull the drawstring to make it fit snugly. Tie the drawstring into a bow.

6. Make the other moccasin the same way.

7. The toes of the moccasins can be decorated by gluing on colored macaroni beads (see pages 28 and 29).

Jewelry

Indian women, and men too, loved to wear lots of bright-colored jewelry. They used shells, animal teeth, and bones to make necklaces.

salt clay

There are several ways to make jewelry for yourself. With salt clay you can make beads of many different shapes.

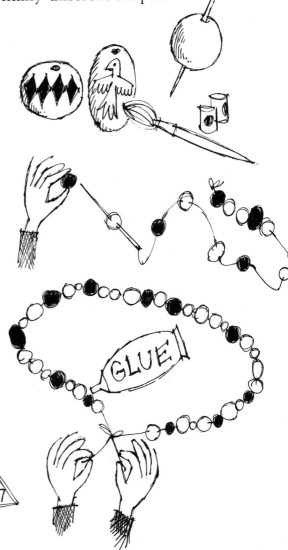

1. Shape the beads from the clay and make a hole through each one with a toothpick. Let the beads dry.
2. Paint the beads. Try putting a design on some.
3. Thread a needle with a piece of heavy thread or colored yarn that is long enough to go around your head with four inches left over. String the beads.
4. Space the beads along the thread. Put a drop of glue in the holes in the beads to hold them in place. Let the glue dry. Tie the ends of the thread in a tight knot.

27

macaroni

Macaroni comes in different sizes and shapes. The small tubular kind is best for making jewelry. You will also need several different shades of food coloring.

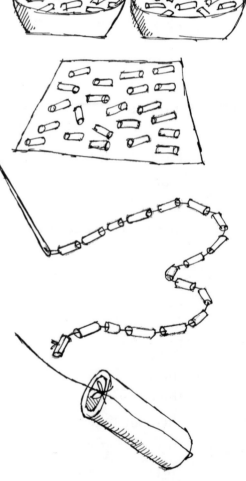

1. Put a little water into several small dishes. Add a little food coloring—a different color for each dish—and some macaroni. Stir the macaroni. Macaroni dyes quickly and it is best not to leave it in the water too long as it gets sticky.

2. Spread the colored macaroni on newspaper. Separate the pieces so they will not stick together. Let them dry.

3. Thread a needle with a piece of heavy thread that is long enough to go around your head with four inches left over. String on one macaroni bead and tie the thread around it. This will keep the other beads from slipping off the end.

28

4. String on the other beads and tie the thread ends in a tight knot. Make several strands of these beads. The more you wear, the nicer they look.

corn

The Indians used corn in many ways. One thing they used it for was making jewelry.

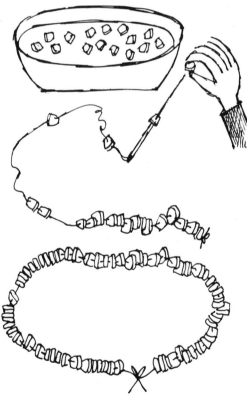

1. Soak a double handful of dried corn kernels overnight to make them soft. For colored corn beads, add food coloring to the water.

2. Thread a needle with a piece of heavy thread that is long enough to go around your head with four inches left over. String on one kernel of corn and tie the thread around it.

3. String on the rest of the corn and tie the thread ends in a tight knot. Put the necklace aside to dry.

Cradle Board

Indian women carried their babies on cradle boards. They took great pride in having these beautifully decorated. The cradle boards were lined with soft, dry moss, which served as a diaper for the baby.

To make a cradle board for your doll, you will need a piece of cardboard. The side of a cardboard carton is fine.

1. Hold the cardboard up to you. If it is wider than your body, trim it. It should be long enough to reach from your shoulders to your waist.
2. Lay the cardboard on a piece of cloth. An old sheet will do. Cut the cloth two inches larger than the cardboard.
3. Fold two inches of the cloth down from the top. Sew this to make a hem.
4. Crayon an Indian design on the cloth.

5. Cut a strip of cloth long enough to go around the back of your neck and under your arms for a shoulder strap. Or cut three strips twice that long and braid them together to make a strap.

6. Punch a hole at each side of the cardboard near the top. Push the shoulder strap through the holes and tie a knot in each end.

7. Lay the cloth over the cardboard with the hemmed edge at the top. Fold under about one inch on each side and two inches at the bottom.

8. Staple the cloth cover to the cardboard. It must fit loosely so there will be room for your doll.

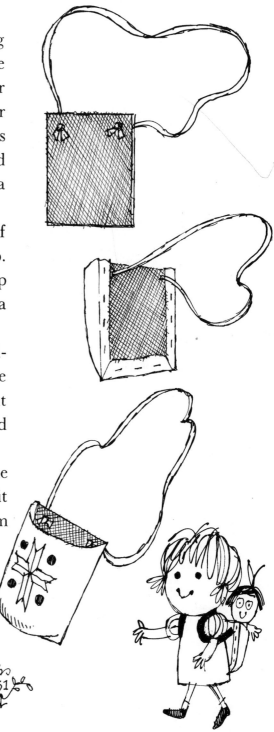

Burden Basket and Tumpline

Indian women used burden baskets to carry corn from the fields and to gather roots, nuts, and berries. They carried these baskets on their backs. The strap which held the basket was called a tumpline. The tumpline fitted across the forehead and over the shoulders.

To make a burden basket, you will need two paper bags the same size.

1. Fit one bag into the other. Trim the edges so they are even.
2. Tape the top of the basket on the *inside* and *outside* with a wide tape. The kind used for taping packages is good.
3. Paint the basket.

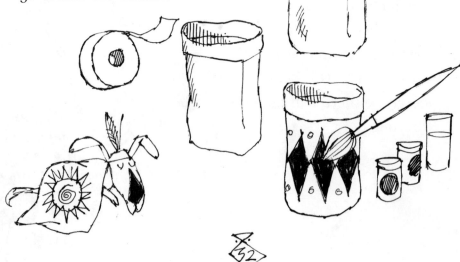

4. Cut a strip of cloth about one inch wide and long enough to fit across your forehead and shoulders as a tumpline.

5. Crayon an Indian design on the strap.

6. Glue or staple the strap to the basket.

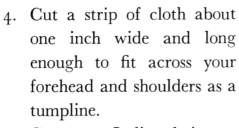

33

Corn-Husk Mat

Indians found many uses for corn husks. They used them as bandages. They braided them to make clotheslines, hammocks for babies, summer moccasins, baskets, and mats.

To make a corn-husk mat, first soak the dried husks from three or four ears of corn until they are soft enough to bend easily. (Green husks can be dried by placing them in the sun for a few days.)

1. Select three long leaves of corn husk and tie them together at one end.
2. Braid the husks. As the ends grow short, overlap a new husk leaf on the short piece and continue braiding.

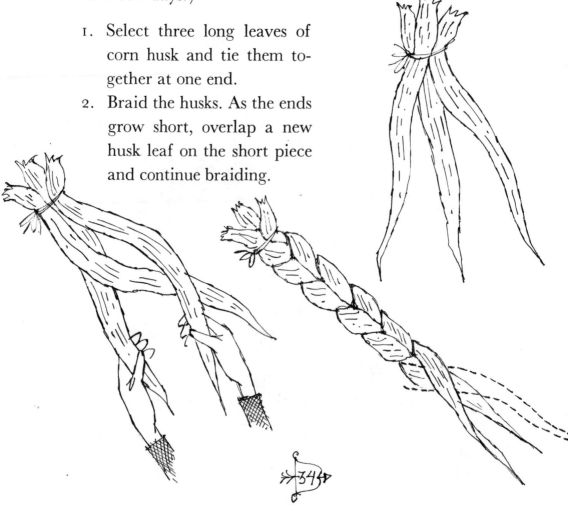

3. Thread a needle with heavy thread. Knot the end of the thread. Coil one end of the braid into a tight circle. Sew the coiled edges together as shown in the picture.

4. Continue coiling the braid and sewing the edges together. When you come to the end of the braid, knot the thread tightly.

5. Place the finished mat between sheets of newspaper. Put several books on top to weight it down so it will dry flat.

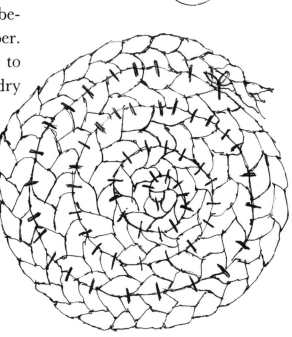

35

Corn-Husk Dolls

The early Indian girls loved dolls just as girls do today. Often their dolls were made of corn husks. Some Indians did not believe in putting faces on dolls. They thought if the doll had a face, it might come alive.

To make a corn-husk doll, first soak the dried husks from one or two ears of corn until they are soft enough to bend easily.

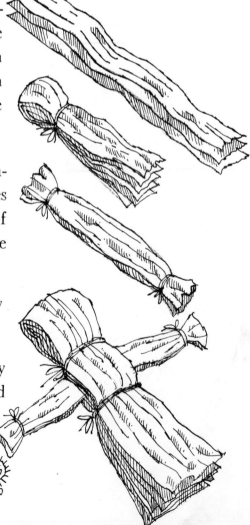

1. Put together three corn-husk leaves that are the same length and fold them in half. Tie a string one inch from the fold to make the head.

2. For the arms, cut two corn-husk leaves about five inches long. Tie strings one half inch from the ends to make hands.

3. Part the husks of the body and slip the arms in place.

4. Tie a string around the body just below the arms to hold them in place.

5. To make a boy doll, follow the same steps. Then slit the corn husks from the bottom to about one half inch below the waist. Tie a string one half inch from the bottom on each side to make feet.

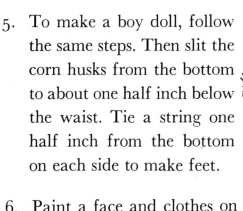

6. Paint a face and clothes on your dolls if you like.

Pottery

Indians made their dishes and pots from clay. They painted beautiful designs on them. Many of the dishes we use today are made from clay.

Perhaps your dollhouse needs new dishes. You can make some just the right size with salt clay.

1. To make plates, take a small piece of clay and press it flat with your hands. Use a bottle lid to cut out the plate.

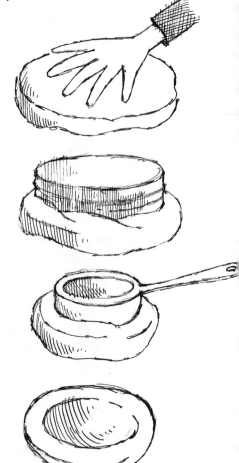

2. Press the round part of a measuring spoon into the plate to shape it.

3. To make saucers, use a small bottle cap to cut out the clay. Shape them as you did the plate.

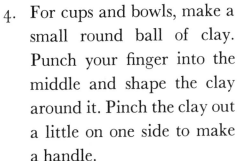

4. For cups and bowls, make a small round ball of clay. Punch your finger into the middle and shape the clay around it. Pinch the clay out a little on one side to make a handle.

5. Make any other dishes you think you will need. Let them dry for at least twenty-four hours. Paint a design on them.

Bow

There were no guns in this country until the white man came. The Indians used bows and arrows and spears for hunting.

To make a bow, you will need a piece of green wood the length you want the bow to be. Green wood will bend easily without breaking.

1. With a nail file or an emery board, file a groove all around the stick about one half inch from each end.
2. Tie a piece of string around the groove on one end. Wrap the string around the groove on the other end.
3. Pull the string until the stick is bent into a bow shape. Knot the string tightly.

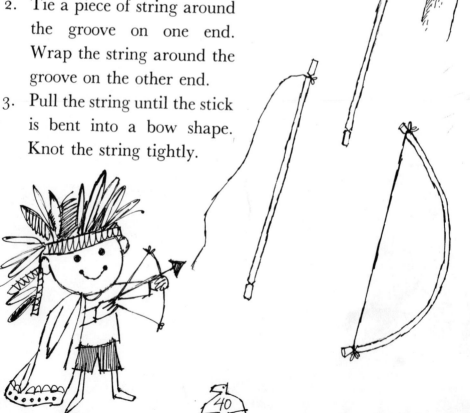

40

Arrows

Indian arrow points were chipped from certain kinds of stone. A feather on an arrow helps to guide it in a straight line. The Indians used goose, duck, turkey, and hawk feathers.

Pretend arrows can be made quickly with paper and sticks.

1. Find thin, straight sticks about one half the length of your bow.
2. Fold a piece of brown, gray, or tan paper in half. Draw arrow points the size you want them. Cut them out. Be sure to cut through both layers of paper.
3. Glue a stick in the center of an arrow point. Cover one side of the matching arrow point with glue.
4. Place the glued side on top of the stick and press the edges of the two arrow points together.

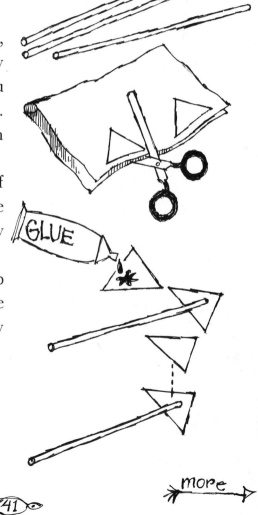

41

more

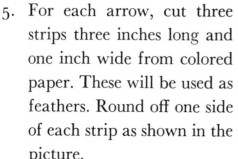

5. For each arrow, cut three strips three inches long and one inch wide from colored paper. These will be used as feathers. Round off one side of each strip as shown in the picture.

6. Fold under one quarter inch of the straight edge on each feather. Put glue along the folded piece. Place three feathers on each arrow as shown in the drawing. Let the glue dry.

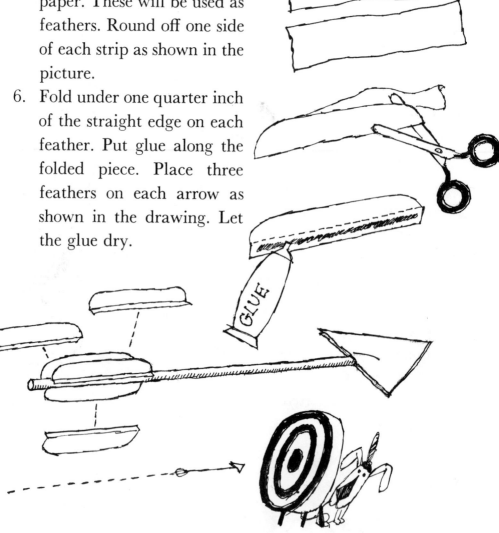

GLUE

Quiver

An Indian carried his extra arrows in a quiver.

Perhaps you would like a quiver to carry your arrows in. You can make one with several full sheets of newspaper.

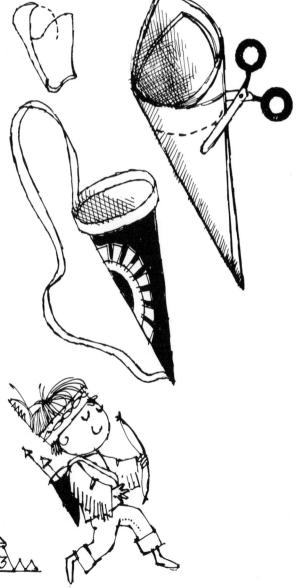

1. Starting with a corner on the folded edge, roll the paper into a cone shape and tape the edge in place.

2. Trim the top even all around. Tape the opening at the top on the *inside* and *outside* with wide tape. The kind used for taping packages is good. Tape all loose edges along the sides and across the opening at the bottom.

3. Cut a strip of cloth long enough to reach across your shoulder and to the opposite side of your waist. Glue one end of the strip to the bottom of the quiver and the other end to the top. Let the glue dry thoroughly and then paint the quiver.

Tomahawk

Most Indian tools were made from stone, shells, or bones. One axlike tool was called a tomahawk. This was also used as a weapon.

To make a tomahawk, first find a thin, straight stick for the handle.

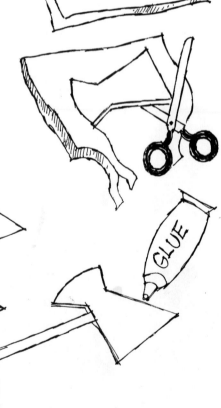

1. Fold a sheet of heavy brown or gray paper in half. Art paper is good for this. Draw an axhead on the paper.
2. Cut along the lines you have drawn. Be sure to cut through both layers of paper.
3. Glue a paper axhead to each side of the stick.
4. Glue the edges of the axheads together.

Shield

An Indian warrior was very proud of his shield. He believed it possessed magic powers to keep him safe. The shield was made from tough buffalo hide.

The side of a cardboard carton makes a good base for a shield.

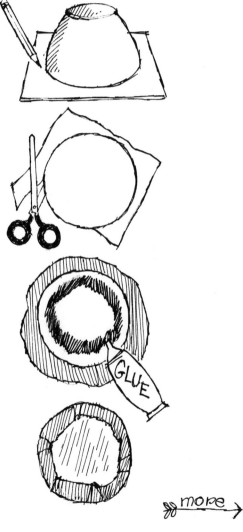

1. Using a large salad bowl or anything else big and round for a pattern, draw a circle on the cardboard. Cut out the circle.

2. Place the cardboard circle on a piece of cloth and draw a slightly larger circle around it. Cut this out.

3. Lay the cloth flat and place the cardboard circle in the center. Spread glue around the edge of the cardboard circle. Pull the edge of the cloth over the cardboard and press it onto the glue. Let the glue dry.

more →

4. Paint the cloth side of the shield brown. When it is dry, paint on a bright design.

5. Glue a piece of elastic or a large rubber band to the center of the back so the shield can be carried on your arm.

Musical Instruments

Indians had many celebrations at which they danced. They used drums and rattles to make their music.

drum

An empty round carton makes a good drum.

1. Tape the lid down. Paint the carton a solid color. When the paint is dry, add Indian designs.

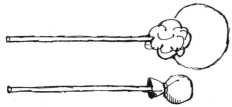
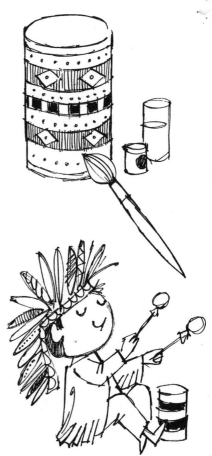

2. Find two straight sticks to use as drumsticks. Put cotton around one end of each stick. Wrap a circle of cloth over the cotton. Put a rubber band around the bottom to hold the cloth and cotton in place.

rattle

An empty round carton also makes a good rattle.

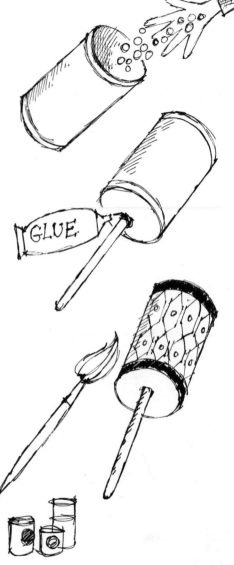

1. Put some pebbles or dried beans in the carton. Tape the lid down.

2. Use a straight stick as a handle. Make a small hole in the middle of one end *or* one side of the carton. Slide the stick into the hole. Put glue around the stick where it goes into the hole to keep it in place.

3. Paint the rattle a solid color. When the paint is dry, add Indian designs.

Masks

The Indians believed that illnesses were caused by evil spirits. To cure an illness, the medicine man danced around the person who was sick, singing a chant and wearing as scary a mask as possible. He hoped this would chase away the evil spirits.

Indians wore masks for many of their ceremonial dances.

To make a mask, first find a paper bag large enough to fit over your head.

1. Cut out holes for your eyes, nose, and mouth.
2. Paint the mask any way you like.
3. Glue on pieces of colored yarn or feathers for decorations.

Wampum

Indians did not have coins and bills for money as we do today. Wampum beads were probably the closest thing they had to our money. These beads were made from the dark purple and white parts of certain shells. The purple beads were more valuable than the white. Sometimes the Indians made beautiful designs on belts with wampum beads. If one tribe wanted to tell another tribe they wished to be friends, they would send a messenger with one of these valuable belts as a gift to the chief.

The kind of macaroni used for jewelry is just the right size and shape for wampum beads. Use the macaroni as it is for white wampum.

1. Mix red and blue food coloring in a little water and dye some macaroni to make purple wampum.

2. Make strings of purple and white wampum to use as money.

3. Make a necklace of purple and white wampum to use as a gift to a neighboring chief or to show your great wealth.

50

Indian Models

Indians of the Plains

Miles and miles of gently sloping hills covered with grass were found in one section of our country. There were no forests there and very little water. But still the Indians found a way to live.

Upon these grassy plains, thousands and thousands of buffalo grazed. The Indians found that the buffalo could supply almost everything they needed to live. The buffalo meat furnished food. The bones were made into tools and weapons. The horns were made into spoons, ladles, and cups. The hoofs were boiled to make glue. The skins were used for clothing and sleeping robes.

But the buffalo did not stay in one place. They moved around, looking for food and water. The Indians had to go where there were buffalo. So these Indians needed homes they could take with them. They lived in tepees made, of course, from buffalo skins.

tepee

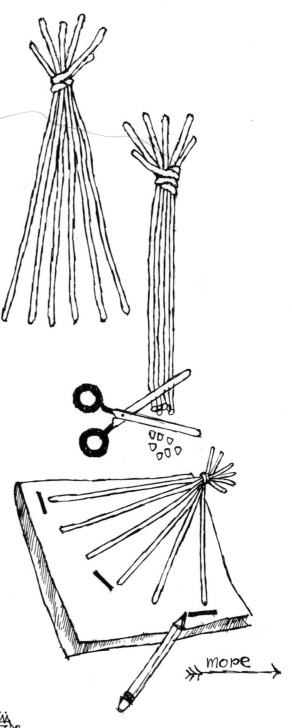

1. Use six pipe cleaners as poles. Twist them together at one end about an inch from the top. Pull the pipe cleaners together at the bottom and trim the ends to make them even. Pipe cleaners can be cut with ordinary scissors.

2. Fold a sheet of paper in half. Lay the poles along the folded edge of the paper so that the twisted part is just above the upper edge of the paper. Mark the length of the straight part of the poles in three places as shown.

more

3. Draw a curving line to connect these marks. Cut along this line. Unfold the paper and you have a half circle the correct size to use as a pattern for a tepee cover.

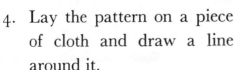

4. Lay the pattern on a piece of cloth and draw a line around it.

5. Remove the pattern and cut along the line.

6. Spread the pipe-cleaner poles to make a frame. Put glue on the *outside* of the poles from where they are twisted to the bottom.

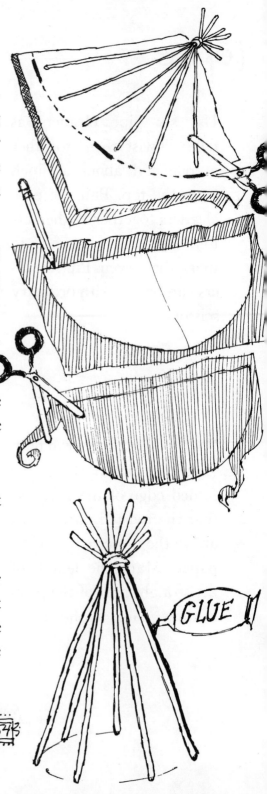

GLUE

7. Lay the cover, *round* side at the bottom, around the frame and press it to the glued poles. There will be an open place at the top of the front for a smoke hole. Glue the ends of the cover where they meet.

8. Cut a slit in front for a door. Fold the flap back and glue it in place. Glue a flap on each side of the smoke hole. The Indians adjusted these flaps so that the smoke would rise straight up and go out the hole.

55

Travois

Travel was not easy for the Indians of the plains. There were no horses in this country until the white man came, and Indians did not know about wheels. The only tame animals they had were dogs. So the dogs were put to work. They were harnessed into an "A"-shaped carrier called a travois, on which bundles were strapped. A dog could pull a load of about forty pounds.

1. Twist two pipe cleaners together about one half inch from one end. Spread them about three inches apart at the other end.

2. Fold a pipe cleaner in half. Slip the looped end around one side of the frame and twist it in place. Bring the ends across to the other side of the frame and twist them around that.

3. Make a small dog from salt clay or peanuts (see Peanut Puppets).

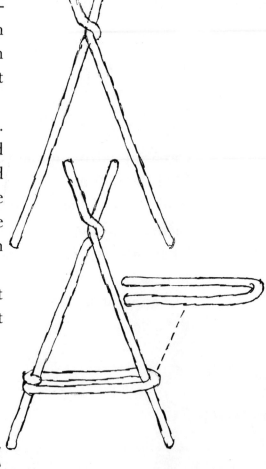

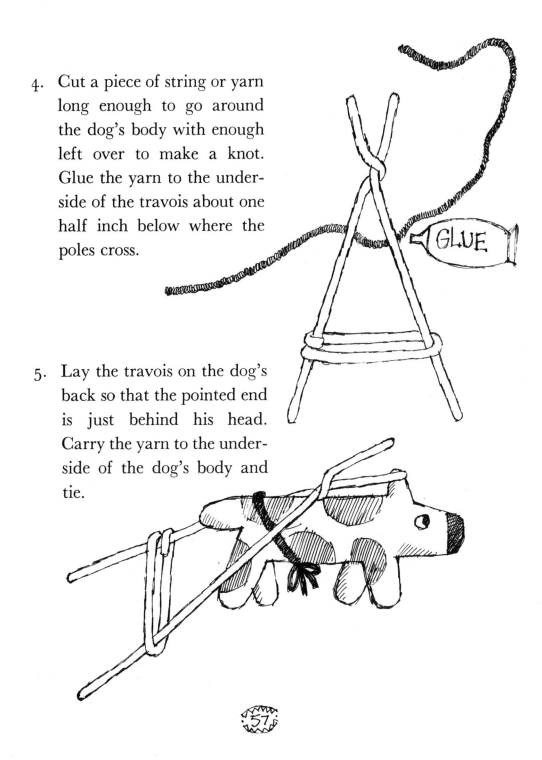

4. Cut a piece of string or yarn long enough to go around the dog's body with enough left over to make a knot. Glue the yarn to the underside of the travois about one half inch below where the poles cross.

GLUE

5. Lay the travois on the dog's back so that the pointed end is just behind his head. Carry the yarn to the underside of the dog's body and tie.

Drying Rack

The Indians went on buffalo hunts only a few times a year. They killed enough buffalo on each hunt to last many months. The meat was cut into long, thin strips and hung on racks to dry. Meat dried this way could be kept for several years and still be good to eat.

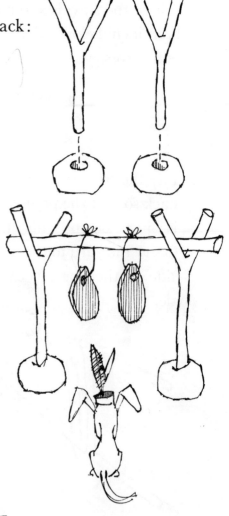

To make a model of a drying rack:

1. Find two sticks about three or four inches long that are crotched at one end. Put a ball of salt clay around the straight end of each to make a base.

2. Stand the sticks about three or four inches apart. Lay a straight stick across the top, letting it rest in the crotches.

3. Make thin pieces of meat from salt clay. Put a hole in the top of each. When the clay meat dries, paint it dark red.

4. Put a thread through the hole in each piece and tie it to the drying rack.

Cooking Rack

Many of the Indian meals were stews that could be cooked in one pot. Most of the cooking was done outside over an open fire.

To make a model of a cooking rack:

1. Make a cooking rack the same way you made the drying rack, but use slightly shorter sticks.

2. Make a pot from salt clay. Put a hole in each side. When the clay pot dries, paint it.

3. Make a handle for the pot by putting thread through the holes and tying a tight knot in each end.

4. Slip the pot handle over the cross stick of the rack.

5. Make a fire by using twigs for wood and bits of painted salt clay for the flame.

Indians of the Woodlands

Many parts of our country were covered with thick forests through which ran rivers and streams. The forests were filled with animals. The rivers and streams were filled with fish. Indians who lived in these areas got much of their food by hunting and fishing. But they also cleared away the trees and planted gardens. The men did all the hunting and fishing, but farming was considered women's work by the Indians of the woodlands.

With so many trees around, the Indians made most of the things they needed from wood. Their homes were called wickiups. This word was changed by the white man to "wigwam." The wickiup was made by bending poles of green wood to make a rounded frame. Squares of bark were tied around this frame with string made from the inner bark of the basswood tree.

Wickiup

1. Cut four strips of paper one 3/4" quarter inch wide and six inches long. Cut one strip one quarter inch wide and ten inches long.

2. Cross the four six-inch strips in the middle and glue each strip where it crosses. Make a circle with the long strip and glue the ends together.

3. Take each of the loose ends of the crossed strips and glue them to the inside of the circle. This makes the frame for the wickiup.

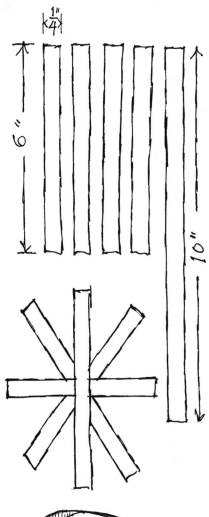

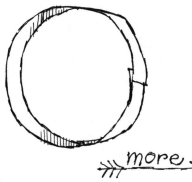

more

4. From brown wrapping paper, cut squares for bark. Glue a row of squares to the frame all the way around the bottom. Have the squares overlap a little.

5. Glue another row of squares above that, overlapping those on the first row. Continue doing this until the frame is completely covered with squares.

6. Cut a door.

7. Leave the wickiup the color it is or paint it brown.

Canoe

The Indians of the woodlands also used wood to make boats. A very light-weight canoe was made from strips of birch bark. The frame was made by bending green branches into a canoe shape. Strips of bark were stretched over the frame and sewn into place with roots or animal tendons. The seams were sealed with pitch, which is the gum from certain evergreen trees.

A canoe was good for long trips because it was easy to paddle and light enough to carry overland from one river to another.

To make a canoe:

1. Press a ball of salt clay into a flat rectangular shape.

2. Fold the rectangular-shaped clay in half lengthwise. Press each end together to make a point.

3. Press the sides out so they are slightly rounded. Press the bottom on the inside to make it flat.

more

4. Shape salt clay around one end of a toothpick to make a paddle. Let the canoe and paddle dry and then paint them.

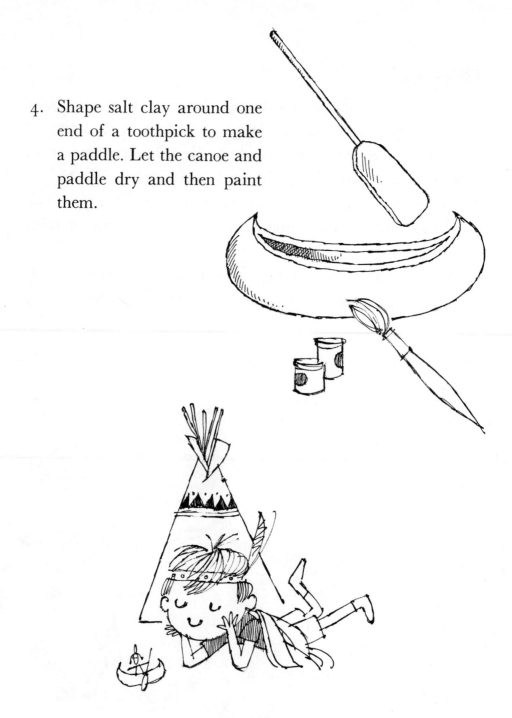

Mortar and Pestle

One of the most important foods of the woodland Indians was corn. They ate corn soup, cornmeal mush, corn pudding, corn bread, and many other corn dishes.

Dried corn was put into a wooden mortar and pounded into meal with a wooden pestle. The mortar was made from a log about three feet high. It was hollowed out at one end.

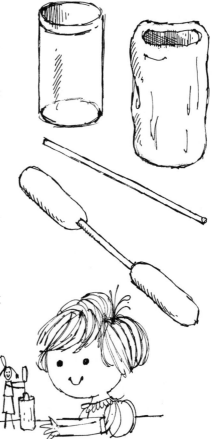

1. To make a mortar, use a small round bottle such as pills come in for a base. Shape salt clay around the bottom and sides.

2. Find a thin stick that is a little taller than the mortar. Shape salt clay around each end of the stick to make a pestle.

3. Let the clay dry and paint the mortar and pestle brown.

Indians of the Desert

Some Indians made their homes in desert land. Water was scarce. There were no trees from which to make houses. There was not enough grass for buffalo, so there were no skins for houses.

But the Indians still found a way to live. There was clay—lots of clay. They mixed clay with dried grass and water to make a mixture called adobe. From this they made bricks to build their houses. Then they plastered the whole outside of the house with a thin mixture of clay and water.

The desert Indians built their adobe houses on flat-topped hills called mesas. They always chose a mesa where there was a river in the valley below. All the water they used was brought up the steep hill from the river.

These Indians were farmers. They hunted rabbit and deer, but most of their food came from their gardens. The gardens were planted in the valley by the river so they could be watered.

Their lives would have been easier if they had built their homes in the valley, but these Indians had many enemies. They felt it was safer to live on top of the mesa. From there they could see for miles around and would not be caught off-guard if the enemy came.

Adobe House

1. Find three small boxes of different sizes that will fit one on top of the other. Cut places for doors in each box. Stack the boxes with the largest on the bottom and the smallest on top. Glue them in place.

2. To make plastering clay, mix salt and flour as for salt clay, but use more water. The clay should be thin enough to spread easily.

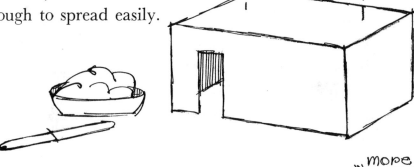

more →

3. Beginning with the bottom box, plaster the outside of all the boxes. Use your fingers or a knife to spread the clay. Make a railing of plastering clay around the edge of the roof. Leave a small opening in the railing for an entrance to the roof.

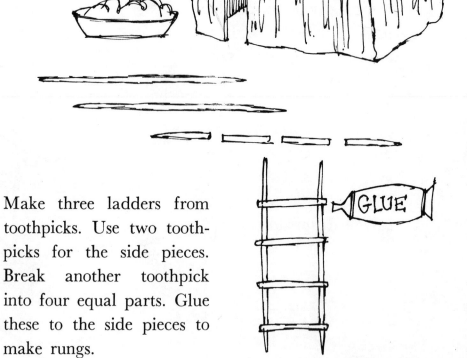

4. Make three ladders from toothpicks. Use two toothpicks for the side pieces. Break another toothpick into four equal parts. Glue these to the side pieces to make rungs.

5. Glue the ladders up the sides from one level to the next. The top ladder should lead to the opening in the roof railing.

6. When the clay dries, paint the adobe tan or yellow.

If you have any plastering clay left over, add more flour to make it into salt clay for the models that come next.

Oven

The women of the desert built large, rounded ovens of bricks and clay. A fire was made inside the oven and allowed to burn until the bricks were very hot. Then the ashes were swept out and loaves of bread were put in to bake.

1. To make a model of an oven such as the desert Indians used, first fold a piece of cardboard in three equal parts to make a base.

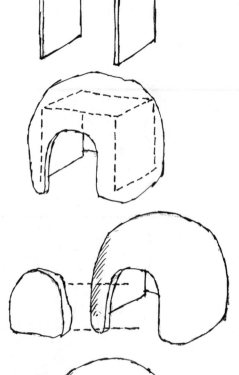

2. Mold salt clay over the base in a rounded shape. Leave an opening for the door.

3. Press flat a piece of salt clay large enough to cover the door opening. The oven doors were not attached, but were held in place by large stones.

4. When the clay is dry, paint the oven tan or yellow.

Metate

The desert Indians grew corn of six different colors—red, blue, yellow, white, black, and streaked. The women of the desert ground their corn into meal on a flat stone called a metate. Meal of different colors was used for different occasions.

1. Press salt clay into the shape shown in the picture.
2. Make a grinder from a roll of salt clay that is not quite as long as the width of the flat piece. Shape the roll as shown.
3. Let the clay dry. Paint a design around the sides of the metate.

Indian Villages

Pipe-Cleaner People

Perhaps you would like to make Indian villages to go with your models. Cardboard cartons, with the top and one side cut off (or just the top), make good frames for these. You can paint in the background you want.

To make model Indians for your villages, use pipe cleaners.

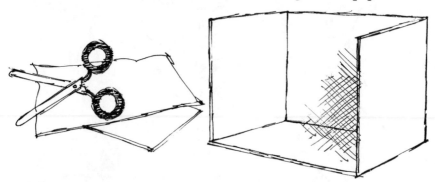

1. To form the head, make a loop in one end of a pipe cleaner, starting about two inches from the top. Twist the end around the main piece to fasten. For the body, make a larger loop with the other end of the pipe cleaner and twist the end in place just below the loop for the head.

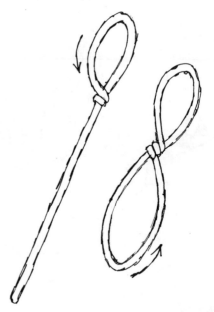

2. Cut two pieces of pipe cleaner for arms and two for legs. Twist them in place on the body.

3. Cut two pieces of cloth or paper large enough to fit the head and two more for the body. Glue a piece on each side of the head and body.

4. Paint the doll brown except for one side of the head, which should be painted black for the hair. Paint on a face.

5. Braid three four-inch lengths of black yarn for hair. Glue the middle of the braid across the top of the doll's head.

6. Glue or tie on clothes.

Plains Indian Village

Paint a background of hills and grass on a cardboard carton from which the top has been removed. Place models of the tepee, drying rack, cooking rack, and travois around the bottom of the carton. Perhaps you will want to model some buffalo from salt clay.

Woodlands Indian Village

Paint a river in the background. Add models of the wickiup, the canoe, and the mortar and pestle. And, of course, you will need trees.

To make trees:

1. Choose sticks with bushy tops for trunks and branches.
2. Tear facial tissues into small pieces and put them in a little water. Add enough flour to make a thick paste and some green food coloring. Mix well.
3. Press dabs of this mixture around the branches of the trees to make leaves. Make a base for the trees from salt or clay.

Desert Indian Village

Paint a background of a valley with a river. Use models of the adobe house, the oven, and the metate. Many kinds of cactus grew in this section of the country. Perhaps you would like to make some for your village.

To make cacti:

1. Twist different lengths of pipe cleaner around half a pipe cleaner.
2. Paint the cacti green. Glue on small, bright-colored paper flowers if you like.
3. Make a base from salt clay.

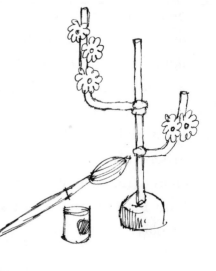

Indian Games

Indian Games

Indians did not work all the time! They loved to play and enjoyed games similar to those we play today.

Here are five games they liked that you may not know.

Cherry Stones

1. For this you will need six cherry or plum stones with one side painted black, the other side white.

2. Decide how many points will make a game. Take turns with your friends to see who can reach game score first. Put the stones in a bowl or box and shake them around. Set the bowl down. If all the stones show the same color, give yourself five points. If five out of six show the same color, give yourself one point. No points are given for less than five of a color.

80

A Tossing Game

1. You will need five peach stones or nuts, each painted a different color. Give a point value to each color and decide how many points will make a game.

2. Use a box or can for the goal and place it on the ground. Make a mark about five feet from the goal to show where the throwing line will be. Try to toss the stones into the goal from the throwing line.

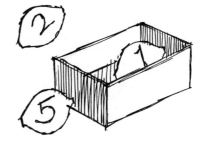

Stick-In-A-Hoop

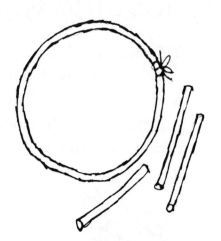

1. Make a hoop by bending a green stick, notching the ends, and tying them together. Find three sticks a little shorter than the hoop is wide.

2. Lay the hoop flat on the ground. Stand about four feet away with your back to the hoop. Toss the sticks over your shoulder and try to get them into the hoop.

3. If you get all three sticks in the hoop, give yourself five points; for two sticks, three points; for one stick, one point.

A Guessing Game

1. The Indians used two identical pieces of bone for this game, but two identical sticks will do as well. Make a mark on one end of one of the sticks.

2. Put your hands behind your back with one stick in each hand and shuffle them around.

3. Make sure the marked end of the one stick is covered by your hand. Put your hands out in front of you and let your friend try to guess which stick has the mark.

Cup-On-A-Stick

For this game, the Indians used a cup made from wood or bark. You can use a paper cup.

1. Find a straight stick about twelve inches long. Cut a piece of string or heavy thread about fourteen inches long and knot one end.

2. With a needle or pin, make a tiny hole in the bottom of a paper cup. Put the thread through this hole so that the knotted end is on the inside of the cup.

3. Wrap the other end of the thread around the stick several times and tie it tightly.

4. Swing the cup around and try to catch it on the top of the stick.

Sand Painting

Sand Painting

The Indians in some parts of the country made sand paintings for use in some of their ceremonies. They made beautiful designs on the ground with colored sand, in the belief these paintings had magical powers that would chase away evil spirits. At the end of the ceremony, the sand painting was destroyed.

Sand paintings can be kept if they are made on paper and the sand is glued in place. Colored aquarium sand can be bought for this, but it is quite simple to make your own from white cornmeal. You can get this in any grocery store.

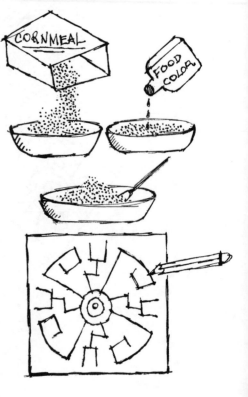

1. Pour some cornmeal into several small bowls. Sprinkle a few drops of food coloring over the meal—using a different color for each dish—and mash the mixtures around with a spoon until all the meal is colored.

2. Draw a design on a piece of paper or cardboard. It is best to try a simple design first.

3. Spread glue on the lines of the design, one line at a time. Sprinkle different colors of cornmeal mixture over the glue. Do not worry about going off the line. Only the mixture that falls on the glue will stick.

4. Let the glue dry. Gently shake off the loose cornmeal.

Peanut
Puppets

Meet Chief Peanut and his wife, Squaw Peanut. That's Papoose Tiny Bird on Squaw Peanut's back. Their other children are Shooting Star and Buffalo Boy. The dog is just called Pup.

Peanut puppets are fun to make. The important thing to remember when sewing peanuts is to sew through the side of the shell away from where it opens. Never try to sew a peanut in the direction the shell opens. For sewing, use heavy thread, doubled, and a darning needle.

1. To make a peanut child, choose a long peanut for the body, a round one for the head, and two the same lengths for the arms and for the legs.

2. Attach the head to the body as shown in the picture. Leave enough thread free at each end to tie off. Tie the threads from the head and body in a tight knot.

3. Knot the thread. Attach the arms to the body as shown in the drawing. Cut the thread about an inch from the arm and tie in a tight knot.

4. Attach the legs in the same manner as the arms.

5. To make a grown-up, follow the same steps through Step 4. Then add another peanut to each leg to make the grown-up taller. Attach as shown in the picture. Leave enough thread at each end to tie.

6. Attach strings to the head as shown. Leave about five inches of thread on each side and tie the ends together.

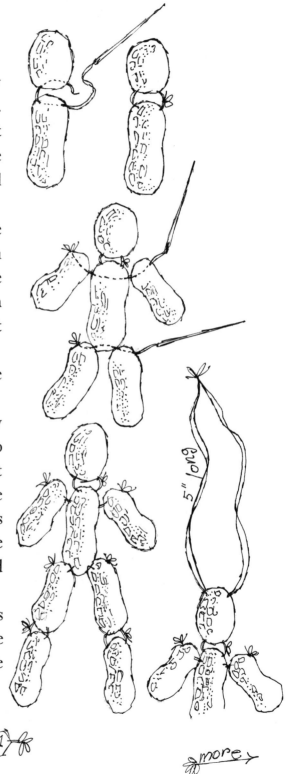

5" long

more

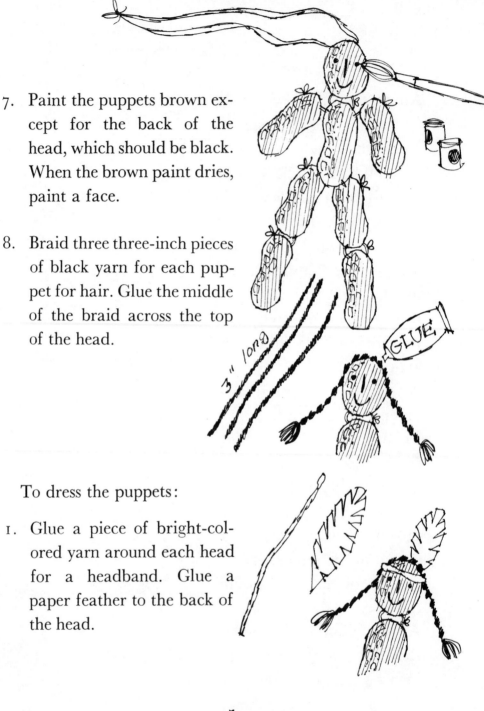

7. Paint the puppets brown except for the back of the head, which should be black. When the brown paint dries, paint a face.

8. Braid three three-inch pieces of black yarn for each puppet for hair. Glue the middle of the braid across the top of the head.

   To dress the puppets:

1. Glue a piece of bright-colored yarn around each head for a headband. Glue a paper feather to the back of the head.

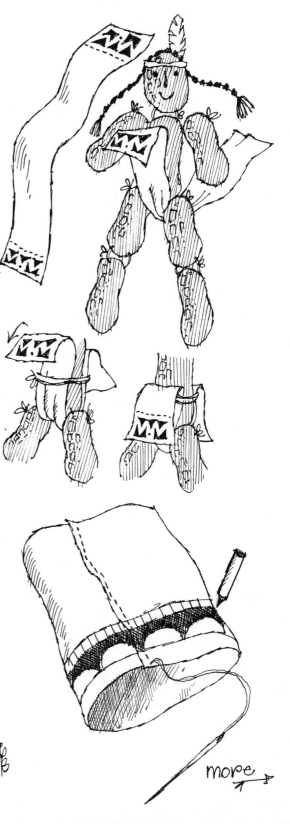

2. Indian men and boys wore only a breech cloth in warm weather. Cut a strip of cloth a bit wider than and twice as long as the body. Crayon a design at each end of the strip.

3. Put the strip of cloth between the puppet's legs and carry it up over the body, with the design on the *inside*. Tie a string around the cloth at the waist to hold it in place.

4. Fold the breech cloth down over the string so the design is on the outside.

5. Paint blouses on the peanut puppets of the women and girls. For skirts, cut a strip of cloth about six inches long and as wide as you want the length of the skirt to be. Sew the ends of the strip together. Crayon a design around the bottom of

more

the skirt. With an unknotted double thread, sew around the top of the skirt.

6. Put the skirt on the puppet and pull the thread ends until the skirt is snugly fitted to the waist. Tie the thread in a tight knot. Glue a narrow strip of cloth around the top of the skirt for a belt.

7. String four or five macaroni beads and tie them around the puppet's neck for a necklace.

To make a papoose:

1. Choose a small, long peanut. Paint a brown face and the rest of the peanut a bright color for a cradle board. When the brown paint dries, paint in the eyes, nose, and mouth, and a design on the cradle board.

2. Glue the papoose in place on the mother's back.

To make a dog:

1. Choose a long peanut for the body, one about half as long for the head, and four of equal length for legs.

2. Attach the head to the body as shown. Leave enough thread at each end to tie. Tie the thread ends from the head and body in a tight knot.

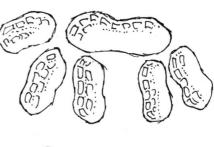

more

95

3. Knot the thread. Attach the legs as shown. Cut the thread about an inch from the body and tie in a tight knot.

4. Cut ears and a tail from paper or pipe cleaner. Glue them in place.

5. Attach strings as shown. Leave about five inches of thread on each side and tie the ends together.

6. Paint the dog as you like.

To finish the puppets:

1. Slip the loop of the thread from the puppet over an ice-cream stick. Adjust the threads so that when you hold the sticks, the puppet's feet are even. Staple or glue the threads in place.

STAPLE HERE

96